More praise for *Series*

"Something quivers in letters," Deweese writes in her new collection. It must be the tension of poetic chords being struck to release their higher lyrical form. The poet is also a musician after all, and so it's only natural that her language finds occasion to sing as syllables dance upon the page. Deweese begins the book by describing an observation of planets as bodies in motion, and we're given to believe that the churning waves created from the celestial spheres that cycle above have persuasion to distort the fine line between madness and love down here on earth. From imagery portraying space as an empty womb to poignant revelations of personal experiences, Deweese has wonderfully woven a balanced tapestry straight from the heart.
— **Scott Thomas Outlar**, author of *Abstract Visions of Light*

Series, by Mari Deweese is a tome of deftly crafted poems centered on themes of time, of the ethereal, of the body. There are whispers in these pages that it is ok to let go, ok to love, more than acceptable to be angry. This collection visits history with language brave and sure, choking lessons out of the fog and dragging them heavily towards the future.
— **Mela Blust**, author of *Skeleton Parade*

Series

from (behind) the Vale

MARI DEWEESE

Nixes Mate Books
Allston, Massachusetts

Copyright © 2021 Mari Deweese

Book design by d'Entremont
Cover photograph by Lauren Leja

All rights reserved. This book or any portion thereof may not be reproduced or used in any manner whatsoever without the express written permission of the publisher except for the use of brief quotations in a book review or scholarly journal.

ISBN 978-1-949279-37-5

Nixes Mate Books
POBox 1179
Allston, MA 02134
nixesmate.pub

"Wenn du mich siehst, dann weine."
Dečín Hunger Rock

In the memory of Frank Deweese, Joe Garis, Kevin Giles, and Michael Wilson. For all of mine that died since March 2020, and also for all the rest. May we be at peace.

Contents

I The Astronomers
Copernicus	3
Galilei	4
Kepler	6
Brahe	7
Halley	9

II Maid/Mother/Crone
To H, O	11
Elizabeth Barrett Browning was a Kinky BAMF	17
Gwynhyfar	20

III Barrie
Hypothetical	24
Pebbles on the Bottom of the Lake Are Rougher than the Ones on the Shore	26
Parathas on Black Lake	28
Hearth	30

IV Logansport
Mound Builders	32
Expectorant	34
Farewell	36
Clockwork	37
Christmas for Franklin	39
Shivervisions on the Hill Slough	41

V	**October**	
	Do Not Pity the Dead, Harry	45
	Is This a Pigeon, or Irony?	48
	Saw Ain, Lamb Bleat	50
	October	52
	Rut	54
	Climax	56
VI	**Dizzy**	
	Prone	58
	'You May Whistle for Me'	60
	In the Arc	62
	I'm looking at you, George Sand	63
	Automaton Swan Song	65
	My Sister is a Trip That Tastes Like CO	66
	Stranger Danger	67
VII	**re: KXXXY**	
	Avoidance	69
	Withheld	71
	Secure	72
	Jugghed	73
	Lance	74
	Aris	77

Series
from (behind) the Vale

Introduction

When I sent in the manuscript for *The Milky Body*, it was a massive collection of mostly things that had been written for a year or more, and that was back in 2018. In fact, it was SO large, I was given the alarming task of splitting it in half. To my fellow writers: Can you feel what I felt in that moment?

How does one decide the best way to skin a cohesive book of poetry, rearrange the guts, stuff it into two NEW skins, and have it make any sense? I had no idea.

So, I began to re-read, and search hard for an answer. And, surprisingly, one presented itself rather quickly in the form of a small, stand-alone series of poems, tucked somewhere in the middle of *TMB*. The Astronomers series existed- and in its existence I realized how I would accomplish the impossible: I would pull out pieces with a common (if obscure) theme that connected them, and see what happened.

And what happened was the rest of the Series. Some were easier to coagulate than others (both Barrie and Logansport are location-specific), and some were exhausting to determine what made a Series and what remained in the official *Milky Body* manuscript.

It was the October series that helped me decide the new structure of *TMB* (I apparently write A LOT about autumnal things) so what did not stay in the series became the Autumnus "chapter". Once I had collected 7 series, I began to organize the remaining poems by season, some sense of something elemental and unseen tying them together.

And then it was released, in 2019, the second half first, because it retained the name, a slippery Jacob to the hairy Esau that is *Series from (Behind) the Vale*. It is my hope that any who have made it to this point in the story read or will read *The Milky Body*, as, truly, the two are one, different sides of the same coin.

Now, I shall quit stalling and let you trip into the vast unconscious that lies somewhere behind the veil that poetry IS –

the dark matter-
the only matter.

1 : The Astronomers

Copernicus

Some nights
I wonder if
some day after
all of your gazing
at these figures
at these bodies
you will still remember
when I was the sun
and you
were the world
at my center.

Galilei

I watch the ripples as a trillion
watch, have watched. But they
don't see you in the middle, pushing
out with unknown density
the ever-closing water, and I do.
And they could not see me,
the shadows on my face, the way
I moved when the sun was on me,
turning me in its arms as a heart
on a spit and burning, but
you caught a glint
 somehow, and thought:
what if I look towards this light?

And you did – and so saw me
fill your eyes full, phasing
into slivers and then to full
again, the first to see me dance,
to tell me: it's ok

to dance while you are on fire –
all the best ones do.
Now a million eyes know
where I am, and I know,
I remember,
they would never have known
what to look at without you
pointing your scope at
me, a speck
in this sky of ink.

Kepler

You stole the charts,
O son of Mars,
and found my roundness
illusory.
Now
exposed, you
see lips: is
my nakedness enough
after all these years
for you to find me
still inside
your firmament?

Brahe

They say
It's just a disturbance
            in the universe. There's
only
the unusual to disrupt
        order in the spheres, orbital
                consistency reveals
the inconstant as fleeting.
        And revolutions continue
as, without lens,
I observe
        you, meticulous,
observatory,
sniffing through verdigris to
pinpoint in the exact
        nature of eruption what
exists outside this closed system,
and what lies inside
        you traced as ley-

lines across my body, so familiar
with the many forms
             within the arc of my ecliptic
you can touch
your tongue to
the precise minute
             I'm halfway to zenith.

Halley

There is always a returning. Periodically.
If whispers woven portend auspices,
if calendrical calculations may
be quantified, if water
gets to be other
than water,
and if a
fire
may
blaze
from ice,
then I expect,
as I believe there's
always a returning, that
when you come around again
(for we get two chances) I will go
with you, flying into the outer darkness.

II : Maid/Mother/Crone

To H, O

So here I am
waiting, holding onto
only what I know for fact
lest confusion over what I don't
smothers me and I falter.

My breath hesitates, lingers as it flows
over and under the slopes of my lips –
it seems to get stuck as it slides
over the lower –
it halts and it throbs and then shudders on in,
and the intake of air shocks me,
as my lungs remember their function.

And maybe, perhaps,
country matters are no such thing
that I should know of, or of which
we should converse, but sir,
your head twixt my legs keeps all focus

at bay, and the nunnery
of which you speak seems
 not so nice a place to dwell as
your mouth
when you speak to me, or
your glance as it falls on me, or
your bed as you...
                              ...drive me mad, you do!
I'm stretched like twine and you keep striking
at my tension, keep trying
to make me sing, but –
if you want me to sing, I'll do it only for you, so –
do you really want me to?
Your tokens, your words beguile me.
Your exhalations of sweet sound
and soft breath tell me that I want
to suck them from out your lungs
and into my own.

No
stone, no

rock, no granite
cage can confine your mind,
or mine, nor can they withstand
the ravages of time, so why should I?
       Soon I will crumble into
             dust as well as you,
                    my lord.

If I could only feel that fire again, that reason-
eating heat! Only feel that sharp beat
of my pulse, in my chest,
in my belly, in my head, filled
with nonsense like...

And I'm wondering WHY
you get so aching
close to my face and yet, with a mere
feathers-breadth between us,
you still won't let yourself
go
won't let
yourself forget, won't let your hands

grab my face and pull it,
like we both know you want to,
to yours so you can taste,
and fully, my budding
insanity with your tongue.

I need that flame; I need that fire.
I need the fierceness that comes
with that need, comes with that love
MY love
and I need to be real, and open,
for your fancy to take flight
through me to make this silence, this
simple compliance, break and release
and float and be free.

Just don't leave me here (where are you now?)
alone and without your light, with only
this
vacant lot of my heart again,
a hollow made bigger by
your invasive fingers,

intruding affections, prodding words –
the hollow now stirred to swirling-colored dark
as the mist creeps in,
conceals the sun, and makes
everything apparent
in its dead little way – I will surely go mad!

And how dare you move me!
How dare you awaken the woman
I never will be and speak to her
of secrets she will never know?
This sorrow seeps
contagious and the deeper,
the harder it is for me to cope –
you are all that I want
to deal with this sadness, all
that I want to deepen
the dark that surrounds this head
and immerse me so wholly in
the memory of
your musky scent.
But –

until then, I'll wear my rue
in a different sort of way,
and when next we meet, my never-love,
take care not to pity me.
I only wish you could see me now,
as I am floating like a vision
of wild violets in the sky,
as I soak, as I slip,
as I sink into, under,
and you kiss me at last!
You are kissing me! now!

Let my lovelogged dress
to the mud take me

down

Elizabeth Barrett Browning was a Kinky BAMF

What matter to me?
(no matter)
Their star is a world.
Mine(…)

Stand further off
then, lost saints
tell me. courtyard wanderers.
Mine has opened (I lived with visions
For company).

In the house of my father
I languished in greyness
laced up, scratching at throat,
certain of only: I will die and here
and soon and slightly. Damp.
I moulder in taffeta.
I do not wait

for a kiss that will never come
from a human mouth. Man's dreams
if bested by God's gifts still leave me cold
dinner for graveworms.

Something quivers in letters.

I have not spent my tears.
They do not collect in a bottle.
The bottle is me.
Some day I'll drown and then

When the fire dies down
what the fuck ya gonna do?

We stand erect, to touch tips lengthening,
mounting
and angels press on us.
 Damn,
 it feels good to be a...

Let me count the ways.
Depth.
Depth.

Depth.
Hey yo Death.
Bosom-swell this, bitch.
Peace.

Gwynhyfar

1.

Great bear in the sky,
Kill me. I beg of you.
I can't bear to look
at tomorrow. the echo
of that tongue inside
the rim that broke
my kingdom, crushed
my womb speaks only
death within this chalice
no matter what slaves
may whisper in their
dim borrowed chapel.

2.

Incessant scratchings at the door,
tappings on the window, clatter like
all the green glass at the bottom

of the closet, saying
dance with me
dance with us!
all the tangy voices
call you coward call
you angry and you answer
fuck you all –

smashed slices like
citrus floating over eyes
heavy smiling from numb
lips tasting berries from
winter, coniferous

– is the place
you try to swim to
speculating or postulated
inside below where they call you from,
from deep daring
dance with us!
sway with mitochondrial
intention, kelp forest climber!

you, with seven ways to fly
if you talk backwards
while you dream of talking backwards
while you fly into the mouth
of the greenest
fattest larvae ever seen: it's
screaming.

3.

Infinitely I
digress.

4.

In cloisters under mound
of bones of secrets find
me sackclothed and round
with babe though i am blind
and old, withered as rind
of orange left out too long
on sill, forgotten, then found.
I only know the one song.

III : Barrie

Hypothetical

I knew I'd most likely never afford that Airstream,
but I also knew, one way or another, some peeling bus
or dubious van would be gutted for pleasure
and utility. And driving, down I-40, orange glow
of westward sun making happiness seem real
as the laugh lines in my face, I would look over
at you, and tell you everything,
about all the years that did not dim
the pain you said I would forget,
about how hard my course had changed,
my stars shifted, how one or two blew up
out in the blackness, but by god
I never let a little thing like direction stop me –
we still and always will know the way home,
after all, don't we? –
and you would laugh, your eyes as bright
with mischief as they ever were, a quirk
in the corner of your mouth as you sighed,
turned your face back toward the road,

letting me go on in the knowing you're gone,
you'd been gone,
aware you only existed in the wreckage
left of my head, grief and madness going
as well together as we ever did, knowing
that you were wrong,
that sorry would never,
could never make up the difference to me,
hands on the wheel,
in love, alone, and mad,
streaming down the asphalt
like it was the sky and I
an actual pilot trying to break
the sound barrier to hear your voice again
beyond the atmospheric haze, somewhere
out in the blueness of this world.

Pebbles on the Bottom of the Lake Are Rougher than the Ones on the Shore

Nothing like a run for a second dose
of emergency contraceptive to signal the brutal onset
of post-party depression once I'd crossed back
over the border. And bleeding
two weeks early becomes a symptom of both
severe chemical imbalance,
and happiness, each cherry drop in the bowl
like the end of a sentence that would still have ended,
but with a more abrupt sort
of punctuation otherwise.
The bruises on my lips fade
faster than the ones left on my legs,
but the imprint of a ghost on them
wakes me with green light
in paranormal hours and I wish
it WAS a dark figure crouched over me,
instead of the thousand miles

from A to B to send me back to sleep,
a hard ache in my bones,
an inflexible twitch
between hips, a stirring in the middle
so like the putrefaction of a body
left too long without another body
finding a hole deep enough
to throw it in.

Parathas on Black Lake

I wanted to scrape
every bit of the rust-
coloured stain off
the bottom of that skillet more than almost
anything. What i wanted more
was to take it with me
when I left, and to place it,
and a dozen green bottles
and a box of lit matches
in a kitchen that does not exist
and to sit, with my tea,
in my stockings,
and watch you flip something else
with such deft skill, watch it land, toasted
and hot, blistered, in the bottom
of that pan that I wish
I could have

kept and I could not,
all that discoloration
left for another hand
to try to clean, another
one to watch with less
wistfulness than I over the cooking
of an early morning
after-screw snack, wanting
to keep the residue
of this memory for long,
long after the soap
bubbles settled and the crumbs
dissolved in a dark
grey
mush down the trap

Hearth

I see you with a bottle of whiskey
Speaking cryptically
Into the blue flames of our love.
Your spit flies from filthy lips
And hits the heat, evaporates
as hate slips into the space
of your breath. And you beg
for death with the panache
of a thief or a liar, telling
Bold tales to the fire
And weeping when the ashes
go cold as the snow
On my shoulders, bare as the last
flicker of light fucks off
And we stare down the chamber
of these, (our) worn, naked bodies
In the outer, maddermost dark.

IV : Logansport

Mound Builders

A History of Kentucky, illustrated
with engravings, published in 1885,
heavy broken leather worn from
father to son to father to son passed
to the bookshelf in the office, tells
of a race of giants, not of the First
Peoples who were here as thought,
but rather migrants from the South
more closely tied to the Mayans. In
the river valleys they built cities, and
walls, and mounds, great structures
eroded now but still potent with old
mystery. Pressed between at random
intervals, stems and crumpled petals
lie entombed by dust and pages. One
rose, once blush, lays flattened head
on folded letter, inked with assertions,
tokens, vows, gone grey on yellowed
paper, memorial to the actual history.

For years they've piled over the sacred
dead between them, my small giants,
their forgotten, unrestful dead, always
and forever piling.

Expectorant

Everyone congregated around
the picnic table under the pavilion

at the local park, a pretty big turnout
that year for the Cardwell side reunion.

Strange and stranger cousins kept
talking to me, and I, not yet aware

that introverted was an ok thing
to be, kept a smile on to be good.

Until one, chatting with my Father,
looked at me and asked: is she

a daddy's girl? I grinned and blushed,
and hid face on my favorite's leg.

His large warm hand settled on top
of my head and mussed my stillbright

blonde hair up, chuckled to the man,
and answered, No, not really. I looked up.

And looked away, and realized that
the thickness of my love for him

would choke me just as easy as
my hate for Her, and it had to go,

because my hate was going nowhere
and nine was too young to drown

in anything other than water.

Farewell

Bobby Skillet always
had a story to tell,
and at his funeral
a hundred folks
showed up to share
some good'uns
in his memory.
But when his heart
gave out in the darkness,
there was only one story,
and he was by himself
when he told it.

Clockwork

Vig leans forward, wrinklebaggy,
soft and translucent as only
the old are, whittling.
Barelydenimnow overalls, which is all
he ever wears with just the one side hooked,
give all of us always the view of the slackness
of ninety-something man-chest,
toothless gums munching those
pukeorangespongepeanut candies
in between plugs of tobacco wadded
in his jaw, spitting the dark juice that stains
the stubble on his chin into decapitated
milk jugs. He whittles
all day, every single day. Shavings
curlier than pubes cover the porch,
the saggy porch, under the saggy roof,
saturated with all the years he's whittled
away in the shade. His old pocket watch,
hanging from its saggy chain, tells the time

is soon, and soon.
The cedar stick he works on
dwindles, becomes a pointed
thing, and gets tossed into the pile
of thousands, identical in every way.

Christmas for Franklin

Out in the yard, the ancient maple stood
full of black sap, so slowly thick and good.
We drilled the hole. We tapped.
We hung a pail to keep the sweetness trapped.

The sap leaked out for days. And as it fell
in that sweet, sad drip - - - drip, it seemed to tell
of cold, and the slow ooze
of losing what it hurts the most to lose.

The tree died, later, unable to bend
within the violence of tornadic wind.
And the sweet sap that flowed
between us once has ceased. And we grow old.

So if Time tells, the story I've heard told
is Time unties the weakest, strongest hold
of familiar bone
and blood, and leaks out love till we are stone.

But in my heart, a wise old tree will weep
its thick black tears, for sap that will not seep
from hearts that are too dead
to see those tears, or wonder why they're shed.

Shivervisions on the Hill Slough

Dirty palms, filthified
by bad well water, rusted pump
guarding the chimney left to rot
to demarcate the horror
of the house where blood
traveled through veins
and seminal
leavings, leering
patriarchs with fingers gobbling
up the promise
of the new, I wipe my hands
and try
to shake the ghosts away.
Red earth, bean shoots breaking
into the scorch, the old hog house
still stinks.
Scored lines crisscross in curves along
the edge of cleared
ground and bush, poke

stalks bulging scarlet through the green
where we took their heads for sallet.
Mudcaked and duckweeded up to
midthigh, but a gar musta
got the brimbait-
hook is empty on the line.
In the holler where the arrowheads
grow, the old spring still
cries. Tears gather in the hole
to spill into the crick that flows down
to the Harican, which joins up
with the Hill, where I
wait in a nightdress
from my great grandmother, eaten
by wolves and moths
and fire, the water not enough
to wash me clean from all
the dirty palms that came before me.
Wading further into this body I lift
feet and float beyond the Horseshoe
Bend, beyond the Green River,

past the voices of children
hiding under the foundation,
past the fear avuncular,
past the death of innocence nailed
in pieces to the walls of missing
memory, past waking, past sleeping,
into the vast unconscious.

V : October

Do Not Pity the Dead, Harry

Hands within hair. Gasps.
Limbs, sprawled or
configured in coarse salt
doughiness, twisted. Too many
muted tones of light
filter through haze to be certain
now if that tongue inside
that place was yours, or
yours, or yours,
any of all the unfulfillable
faces poking from the
shadows of past fires.
Does she recall
that time going through
the car wash? Son, that's
a lot of history
to sort through. Does she
remember that one night,
in the storm? So many storms, try

another keyword to assist
in the search, perhaps
'October,' 'nature trail,'
'after the show,' or 'before you
beat her face in,' for a quorum.
She may then be able
to peacefully concoct
a memory from scratch
just for you, if she's in a generous
mood, to say, oh yes, I do
remember that now.
But really, truthfully, she does not.
And she doesn't want to,
doesn't need to rent the space
in the wasteland of her head
on intact experiences, complete
with names, dates, addresses,
current world news, what was eaten
or said or not said. The shapeless
feel of the thing is all the memento
she takes with her, because

who really wants to be haunted
by more ghosts than the ones
we already have to carry?

Is This a Pigeon, or Irony?

At 14, menstruation became
a not-regular house guest
and a blooming insatiability for leaving
girlhood behind
took her
one night to her closet where
she popped her own cherry
with a tampon. Glad that's out
of the way, she thought.
Two years down, no further
penetration (save some
occasional digits) touched her
unwanted social construct
until
the night it actually *was* lost, taken
from her crudely
by a shadow unbothered
to remove the cotton plug that screamed
louder than she did

that this one was
not ready.

Saw Ain, Lamb Bleat

There is a veil that hangs
from rings of mythos.
It thins
 (efface and dilate)
and then
thickens
 (pucker
tight) again
once the passengers
have made it
 through.
But
blood will open it
like steel rods
inserted one by one and
 the right blood
(so the myth goes) once split it
nose
to

navel,   (all the glory of)
what gnaws
               from beyond
the grave
    spilt
        out from behind it.
The flood swallowed
an entire generation,
and left
              the (rust)
aftertaste
of corpse
      maggots on
              the tongues
        of all this (sandgrain,
skystar)   world of worlds.

October

is the month
I love to wish
that I loved

is the month
of birthdays
and leaf forts

clementine
sunshine on
forest runs

waking wet
with terror
in darkness

to feel hands
crawling on
me, ripping

my body, and
shoving fear
in my cavities.

Rut

Ungulantic shedding of
the velvet. Shreds rubbed
in frantic on wood, dangling
in bloody strips leaving
traces on trees before.
Lip-curling urine, bending
to ground with swollen
neck, urging and restless.

Cylindrical slipping
and pressing into. Wetness
precipitates, deeper
gorges to be dangerous
when dry, more so
when the suck down pulls
piece into the squish
of lovely muckstuckdom.

In I, migratory ecliptic
forces bright head

lower into skylap.
Less of light I munch
sparse chlorophyll.
Clothes peel as
shudders in the season
lonely: what leaves
remain me burn.

Climax

At the end
of all the feckless
fetid humping
there is still
the squirming remnant
of uneaten eels,

VI : Dizzy

Prone

To misdirect.
To massage an ego
till it suits me
to find myself mistaken.
To leave love hungry.
To tell half-truths, knowing
there are only lies in my throat, knowing
a good spin makes
a good story.
To be ridiculously fertile.
To lose.
To laugh while I'm losing.
To laugh while a wad of spit runs
down my face where he hocked it, like,
what else
are you gonna do that can't touch me?
To do things myself.
To need intervention on the DL.
To taste the taboo just to feel-

Home?
To lie at night unable to sleep.
To wake up face down
on the floor in the AM,
shirt pulled up over my
head, having effed myself
into the only
oblivion I've ever found here.

'You May Whistle for Me'

(for Edna St. Vincent Millay)

It's been so long now
I can't remember
if it was you
or me
who first tightened your belt
around my throat.
I can't remember
who grabbed the end and pulled it
to the back, my head yanked
backwards on its hinge,
if I fell or was pushed
to the floor, if I liked it
because I am dirty
or if I am dirty
because I liked it,
and mostly, I can't remember
at what point

the belt became
invisible,
and I crawled on all fours
to get pissed on
just because.

In the Arc

They told me I was being paranoid,
that the fact that my feet were in flames
and the fire kept crawling up my legs
didn't actually mean that I was sitting
in the exact place where hell decided
to seep through to my reality, because
I was high off my ass. They were right.
I've been in hell since, and not only
my lower limbs, but every part of me,
my mind an inferno, heart incinerated,
body burned till skin slipped off, black
crackling, tongue exploding, melting
eyes, and not a soul could tell me I was
paranoid (not one knew I was on fire)
and not one specter would have wanted
to hazard a mad guess at the gospel: I
got high on the trial, stake-tied, set alight.

I'm looking at you, George Sand

Patriarchy sucks.
Feminism – sucks.
Pants, however, suck
the very biggest
one of all.
The irony of being equal
by dressing in clothes
with designated leg holes
is that now to fuck
I must get at least half-way naked.
The freedom of the bondage
we were told was a skirt
is that it just needs pushed up
over my hips, and I can express
my womanhood
without exposing any more
of my self than my ass.
So for my share of liberation
I will choose to go

pantsless and – fuck panties, too –
1) because i hate that stupid word
and 2) 'cause I enjoy the breeze.

Automaton Swan Song

We seek death as a cervix
to the secrets of the universe.

> Hooks and wires beckon
> > a black hole from the river
> > in my abdomen.

Until the orb slips out of its yellow
> wallpaper skin I gag
> with the glue of a thousand

famine years' ejaculate, nebular
in circular reasoning, busting my jaw

> as dark matter trickles down
> as red as my mouth
opening to release the swarm of locusts
> > sticking
to the roof of my carcass

we will not escape this tunnel vision.

My Sister is a Trip That Tastes Like CO

"That's a nice shirt – is it new?" she asks.
"Thanks. Yeah, it is."
"You sorta look like a bumblebee."
"I was told I looked like a stupid Charlie Brown."
She looks again for a second.
"It looks like if Charlie Brown and a bumblebee had a lovechild…"
I nod in agreement. She continues.
"…that was skinned and made into a shirt."

Stranger Danger

Some thing may indeed
Not love a wall,
But that something isn't me.

There lurks
In wait within the shapes that creep
Away from streetlights, creatures
Hunting for the whiff
Of warm blood.

Lucky for me,
I'm already
Carrion.

VII : re: KXXXY

Avoidance

Can it be helped that these poles now repel?
Or that these subatomic particles particulate together no more?
What can be said when home becomes only a door,
and a mat outside with Wellies waiting on it?

The fireplace hasn't been used in years. I meant
to clean it out last fall, but way leads to way,
and ages have been spent more than sighs
of late. The pillar candles in the grate grow
even more dusty despite my efforts, which are,
I admit, not always the best. The brick needs
to be painted, but I may have fallen in love a bit
with the sad trace of soot that clings to the edge,
and reminds me that there used to be fire here.

(To sweep a floor
in need of sweeping
is one of life's simple pleasures.
[Believe me,
if I believed otherwise,

I would have left
this mess ere now.])

Quantum entanglement can only encapsulate so much
before the longing to be reunited with the disengaged
preys upon what light there may have been
once, on the other side of
some alternate universe in the mind
of a god who left us
floating in the big empty, the iconic scene:
unlucky astronaut
with that cord stretched, stretching back
towards the station, a dark umbilicus in utero suspended
as the fear births itself, with wrinkled pink lungs
pressed against the inside of a depressurized helmet.

Ground Control.
Are you there?
Are you there?

Sssssksksssskskkksksksskkksksksksksskkss

Withheld

Affection or paycheck,
one hurts worse than the other.
In the shade of a broken cypress,
only visible knees offer a place
of rest, ebony and unquiet.
Disaffection releases spores,
which land on the water, and swim
on the current to elsewhere
in my heartsick mind, mired
by my own shady indigence
and an account that never once
has been much for abundance.

Secure

My new yo-yo drops,
Spins, then eats itself again.
Your palm cups softly.

Jugghed

Any boy can wield
the forciest field,
and you have
a shiny helmet
as a shield.
Don't stop, they say
to unstoppable clay –
as if you would yield.
metaphorical force- play
with your rocks
and keep your face
concealed.

Lance

Ergo
The aspens
Shive
r, reeling from a dusk
too humid in nature
for this season. Appetency
lengthens in the shadows
who ripple down the stone
the singing stone
burgeons in ecstasy
of thwartation. Courtly love
is less flirtatious than
curious: MY WEB FLIES WIDE.
Ergo
you are my mirror. The river,
The womb, the warrior,
the curse. I do not exist, but you,
Sun-kissed night, will rise
beyond the prows of all this

crusty understanding
and know my name
if it is the only gift
that I can give you.
Ergo
The wheel spins, the joints
Stretch, and we break
our own bread dipped
in our own vintage for
absolution, exploration, communion
with the three spirits
that hold us in contempt
until the polarity of chivalry
and degeneration slip inside
each other and release seed
to reach two-thirds synthesis
before a spontaneous abortion
in a gibbous phase.
Ergo
The falcon flies towards the east;
The dove flies south;

The moth in the window;
The wax on the casement,
Dripping. Do not let me in.

Aris

Things are the things they are!–
cried the poet, flitting
about the place.
A sea-battle raged in the distance,
which had seemed a likely event
in any case.

Acknowledgments

Certain poems have been featured in *Setu Mag*, and *Three Drops in a Cauldron*. "Galilei" was published as a limited broadside by Nixes Mate.

About the Author

Under the influence of both the River and irreverence, Mari 'Diz/zy' Deweese lives and sings and writes of what she's learned on the rougher, sometimes slicker, side of the Queer American dream in Memphis. When she isn't busy selling whatever sells these days, she releases her work through the blessed small presses, and her artist pages on social media. Her first three books, or 'The Kinky Volumes', from Nixes Mate Books stand as a solid introduction to the rest of the poets, and the rest of what's left.

42° 19' 47.9" N   70° 56' 43.9" W

Nixes Mate is a navigational hazard in Boston Harbor used during the colonial period to gibbet and hang pirates and mutineers.

Nixes Mate Books features small-batch artisanal literature, created by writers who use all 26 letters of the alphabet and then some, honing their craft the time-honored way: one line at a time.

nixesmate.pub

www.ingramcontent.com/pod-product-compliance
Lightning Source LLC
Chambersburg PA
CBHW051807100526
44592CB00016B/2606